A Good Work
BEGUN

Renée Hill Carter

Copyright © 2012 by Renee Hill Carter

A Good Work Begun
by Renee Hill Carter

Printed in the United States of America

ISBN 9781622303175

All rights reserved solely by the author. The author guarantees all contents are original and do not infringe upon the legal rights of any other person or work. No part of this book may be reproduced in any form without the permission of the author. The views expressed in this book are not necessarily those of the publisher.

Unless otherwise indicated, Bible quotations are taken from the New Living Translation. Copyright © 1996, 2004 by Tyndale House Publishers, Inc.; The New King James Version. Copyright © 1982 by Thomas Nelson, Inc.

www.xulonpress.com

Dedication

...

This book is dedicated to my family.

My husband, William (Bill). Your love, support and encouragement
means the world to me. Thank you for constantly urging me on.

My children, William, Jr., LaKeshia and LaChanda, the "fruit of my womb."
You are truly a "heritage from the Lord" that I treasure.

My wonderful grandchildren, Mitchell, Jr., and Kamryn
You two are so amazing. I marvel at you.

To my sister, Georgianna Hill Purnell. You are so precious to me.

I love you all!

...

In loving memory of:

My father, Abram G. Hill
My mother, Margaret L. Hill
My sister, Patricia Hill Ellerbe

Acknowledgements

...

My gratitude to Traci Ethridge of Omni Creative Services, LLC for the cover design and image formatting throughout the book. I truly appreciate all your help and patience in reviving this project.

In this work of art, Renée Carter reveals the essence of her inner most being. While doing so, she touches the depth of God's grace, love, purity, and holiness that we all long to touch. It's no wonder, as you come to know Renée Carter, you will get to know her and the power of her gentle witness for the God she reflects and loves.

Dr. Phillip M. Davis
Founder and Senior Pastor
Nations Ford Community Church
Charlotte, NC

Contents

Prologue xiii

The Struggle	Before salvation 17
What Am I to Do?	Now what? 19
No Time	Don't look back 21
Hidden in Thee	You're safe now 23
A Note	Love letter to God 25
In the Midst of a Blessing	Don't give up 27
Sonrise	All for you 29
Touch the Wind	He'll never leave you 31
Living Water	No whining allowed 33
The Wonder of it All	Can you believe it? 35
Seek to be Alone	Just you & God 39
I Repent	Have faith in God 43
The Great Melt Down	Losing control 45

Young Tender Girl	*Purity* *49*
Love	*Love* *51*
A Story in Progress	*Don't judge…pray* *53*
A Saint gone Home: "The Call"	*He told you so* *57*
A Saint gone Home: "The Exhortation"	*Are you ready?* *61*
Untitled	*Matthew 25:31-46* *65*
The Third Place	*The Mysteries of God* *67*
Dare to Love…Dare to Live	*Live it!* *69*

Epilogue *73*

Prologue

...

Whether you've traveled the globe or have barely ventured past your door step, no journey is as thrilling as the one we're on right now. Life is a marvelous journey. It's even better if God plans your trip from beginning to end.

To see oneself pass from death to life, from darkness to light, from being born to being born again is the beginning of a miraculous journey. The sights and experiences along the way are well worth the trip if the compass of the Holy Spirit is your guide. The final destination is eternal hope fulfilled *"when Christ, who is our life, shall appear, then shall we also appear with him in glory."* (Colossians 3:4)

Take a trip with me now through these pages and let us, together, visit some very interesting places. The journey of the soul can take you to realms of reflection, encouragement, mysteries, awe, introspection, boldness, assurance, hope…

My hope is that God has begun a good work in you and that you will allow Him to take you to the best places on earth and in heaven!

...

"And I am certain that God, who began the good work within you, will continue His work until it is finally finished on the day when Christ Jesus returns."
Philippians 1:6

(New Living Translation)

The Struggle

Trying to touch the darkness
Trying to capture and keep the light
Trying to begin all over again
Trying to enter a new plane
   with the intensity of your birth.
The wind seems to be leaving from your sails
   quickly and without prologue
The struggle is the one thing that seems real.
I am seeking to arrive.

What Am I to Do?

My God, what have you planned for me?

I'm anxious now to know.

Shall I be the one to save this world

   or will I be consumed by it?

Shall I touch just one heart and make it glad

   or will I let the pains of many prevent my efforts?

Shall I cause the birds to perfect that one unsung song

   or will I clip their wings in their flight to Glory?

Shall I utter a kind word

   or keep silent and let my words dissipate for no one to hear?

Will I write a verse to inspire someone to newness

   or still my pen and hoard my thoughts unto myself?

Oh my God, tell me, what am I to do?

No Time

No time to crave sad songs or lost tears

No time to ache and sorrowfully drink from the cup of plenty

No time to wish the pain would return to give reason to mourn

Need a little more time to mourn but no time to…

Time to get up from my death, change my mind and march to the tune of LIFE.

Hidden in Thee

No longer do I hide me in me
Where heartache embraced my being
When flight was my only out
    to be propelled into a loud darkness of ceaseless
    non-direction
Bringing with it acid tears filled with shrilled stings of pain
I would hide me in me and oft' times stay much too long
    only to return to a new depth of despair.

No longer do I hide me in me
I can now hide me in Thee
Where the once darkness is now brillianced with Light
Where triumph is my mainstay
Where quiet, joy and peace are absolute
I can stay at the foot of the Cross until the warmth of
    your Son lifts me soaring to yet another height…

No longer do I hide me in me
Thank you Father, I can now hide me in Thee.

A Note

Just a note to you Lord
To say to you just how
The knowledge of your love
Is overwhelming me right now.

To tell you just how much
Your presence means to me
To say to you my Master
How precious it is to be.

Your child dear Heavenly Father
A vessel of your clay
To be at your disposal
To live within your way.

So Lord above please listen
To my heart as it beats to say
I'm glad to be your vessel
I'm with you now to stay.

In the Midst of a Blessing

I at times find myself in the midst of a blessing.
Though it tastes like vinegar,
    it becomes as honey to my lips.
Though it pricks like a thorny thistle,
    it becomes as smooth as a rose petal.
And though it causes me to shiver in its coldness,
    it embraces me with HIS warming touch.
Though clouds hover 'round my head,
    it brings forth the SON in all HIS glory.

So let me be still and praise my Lord and
Rejoice in the midst of my blessing.

Sonrise

Wash you in the water of His tears

Bask you in the golden Son of His rising

Adorn you in His garments of silk

Take all that He has for you

Eat all that He has prepared for you

Run the race that He has said you will win in His name

Then lay your head on His shoulder and

He will give you rest.

Touch the Wind

When you feel it matters not
What you say or do
Just remember the Lord above
Is always loving you.

When you think your caring tears
Have been shed in vain
Just look up and see Him there
He's smiling through the rain.

When this world makes you feel
That no one's there to care
Touch the wind, hear His song
His Spirit's always there.

When you need a listening ear
Your secrets to confide
Go with peace inside your heart
Therein God does abide.

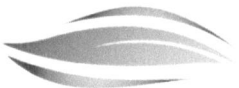

Living Water

How dare we continue to whine
When there are those who have the right
To wail without ceasing deep into the night.

Why do we insist on not seeing the
    shimmering light of Hope
When there are those whose eyes are clouded
    with cataracts of despair
Yet they beg to see.

Who among us have seeds of our being made
    manifest and don't rejoice at their touch
When there are those whose barren wombs
May never feel the flicker of life within.

Quickly! Let us hasten to drink from Your
    goodness overflowing
For fear that they may choose to die of thirst.

The Wonder of it All

My finite mind cannot contain the wonder of it all
On my own I tried so hard to find my earthly call
But then a Voice from heaven kept ringing in my ear
"Child of the dust, be still awhile the answer is very near.

I AM THAT I AM, Jehovah God is my name
Father, Son and Holy Ghost, we're all One and the same
It's way past time that you and I settled on this score
I AM God, there is no other, need you something more?

My Voice is still, my Voice is quiet, in it there is no doubt
Don't you think that you should see what Living is all about?
I sent my beloved Jesus to give you abundant life
In the midst of pain, death, confusion, hate and strife.

So hear my Voice through My Spirit, I'm speaking just for you
Don't you try to figure this out, just believe that it is true
By faith you must come to me believing I AM He
The one who died to give you life to live eternally.

So come to me just as you are, your burdens give to me
For you only the best will do, won't you taste and see
That I AM sweet, I AM pure, I AM rich in grace
I ask you now never again from me hide your face.

Ask of me, seek after me, knock on my Door
Open up your heart you'll see I have so much more
More than you could ever imagine in your finite mind
Golden riches, treasures untold only in Me you'll find."

Seek to Be Alone

Loneliness is not really alone
For loneliness is fraught with company
With fullness, with a legion of vanity and emptiness
With busloads of fears, of overnight guests
    whose stay is overdone.

Loneliness is not really alone
For loneliness is replete with gods,
    gods with dumb mouths, stopped up ears
    gods whose loves have limits,
    gods who can't hear your tears.

Loneliness needs to be alone
For to truly be alone you get a glimpse of God
Loneliness yearns to be alone
For only then can ears be attuned to His Voice.

Loneliness hungers to be alone
For then you can taste and be filled with His Goodness
Loneliness must be alone
For then to His touch you can yield

In His bosom you can rest
To His house you can go
And stay forever.

Seek to be alone with God.

I Repent

If I am to walk by faith and not by sight
Then I must hate anything that is not of faith
For it is sin.

If I am to have no other gods before You
Then I must tear down the idols of selfishness
   erected by my hands
For that too is sin.

If I am to lay aside the weight that impedes my stride
Then I must do so with the strength of Samson
If not, it becomes sin.

If I am to put away the sin that doth so easily beset me
Then I must hate it with perfect hatred
For not to, is sin.

You love me with perfect Love beyond eternity
You allow me to partake at Your Supper table
You give me your Spirit to do what must be done
To ignore that for a moment is sin.

Forgive me Lord.

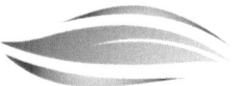

The Great Meltdown

Watching me dissolve into nothing
Emptying me of me to make ready for that
   great invasion
Of all my privacy, of all my self
Is all consuming
As well it should be.

Watching me melt into oblivion
Purging my once sense of well being and
My wonder of self delusion and vain filled glories
Is a welcomed gift from above
As well, it ought to be.

Watching Jesus take shape in me
Creating in me this new creature by
His perfect hand of eternal wisdom
Is a mandate of grace
As well it must be.

Watching this miracle of my new birth

Set the pace for His marvelous Life to grow in me

For His smile to be mine

His touch to linger forever

His power unleashed through me

Is not of this world

As well it can never be.

Young Tender Girl

She believes in flowers and rain
In soft sketches of men and women,
   boys and girls, wistfully set upon the canvas.
She holds in her heart breezes singing
   songs of sachet rainbows.
She believes in God's smile of golden rays
   upon our heads.
Her soul and sweet mind ignite at the
   beauty of God's greenness and at the
   feel of soft kitten touches on her face.
Her sonata is full of perfect harmony and hushed
   silence sprinkled with tones of peace and love.

Love

You are Love.

You give succulent sweet

You are the nectar of my soul

    that I can taste anywhere.

My Love.

A Story in Progress

Be careful how you shake your head
    when you see somebody down in squalor.
God just might be in the making of a good story.

Be mindful of what you think
    when you see somebody doing things "you'd never do!"
God just might be thickening the plot.

Be real sure you know what you're doing
    when you wash your hands of folk when they don't do to suit you.
God just might not have revealed the conclusion yet.

Be very, very quiet when you keep talking about
    how you're through praying
Because they won't ever change.
God just might be about to release another of His best
    sellers.

Fine tune your spirit

Unstop your ears

Look through the eyes of the One who saved you

Then bow your head

Because God just might be working on another masterpiece.

Be still and see the salvation of the Lord.

A Saint Gone Home

The Call

Jesus made a call
Just the other day.
The message from the MASTER said
It's time to go away.

To your golden mansion
My WORD is always true.
Your place has been made ready
It's waiting just for you.

You did the things I told you
In my precious NAME.
A kind soft word, an encouraging smile
Lives touched won't be the same.

Dear one, I know they love you
But I love you even more.
Let us go to our loving FATHER
He's waiting at the door.

In loving memory of my father, Abram G. Hill
My mother, Margaret L. Hill
My sister, Patricia Hill Ellerbe

A Saint Gone Home

The Exhortation

It's been a little while now
Since Jesus called for me.
The mansion that He said was mine
Is beautiful to see.

But let me tell you this one thing
That surely you must know.
It's so important that you be ready
When it's time to go.

Time is nigh, you can tell
Just read it in His Word.
Troubles and strife are on the rise
These things I'm sure you've heard.

But seek ye first God's Kingdom
And all His righteousness.
All other things will be added to you
If Jesus you first confess.

Open your Bible, study now
Read it everyday.
Don't just hear, but you must do
The things God has to say.

Then tell your brother of the news
Of God's sweet saving grace.
This is the service God needs from you
With patience you'll win this race.

God is doing a new thing
Remember He's in control.
Just be the servant He needs you to be
Make sure you're on the roll.

Untitled

I know absolutely nothing of which I write
I hear the saxophonist's moan
I see them on the street
With that to call home

I can't imagine not being able to go home
I won't
Hypocritically I cry
And then
I go…home

The Third Place

You can stay here or go there

Or seek out the third place

Where you can defuse the bomb

Where doves go to make peace and love

Where you can call You and talk…or not

Where illusion is made real and

Real…illusion.

Dare to Love…Dare to Live

A multitude of experiences, deeds, good and not so
Thoughts, fleeting and staged
Heights, depths.

A series of heart rhythms
So painful at times
So joyful at times
So tumultuous as needing a steady hand to still the discord
   so much a part of it being realized.

A dance of pleasure no one could define but God.
A dance of death to old things whose demise must be
   celebrated in order to live again.
An orchestra of symphonic booms of unrelated events
That somehow manage to meet at the same place, at the
   same time
That only the Conductor could have known
That only the Composer could have written
That only Maestro God could blend to such an ecstasy of
Truth.

And you think you understand Love.

Love is unrelenting

Love is unforgiving in its pursuit of itself.

Of its need to be fulfilled and grow eternally

Of its destiny found only in the eyes of God.

It doesn't quite look like what I was told.

It doesn't quite feel like what I felt at first.

It contains sorrows

It contains the reality of certain truths that one thought could never be.

It takes from you…it must so that it can be free to have room to show the truth of itself.

It's possible that it can't be defined.

It's probable that it can only be lived to be discovered bit by bit.

And then we'll know.

Dare to love…Dare to live.

Epilogue

...

The Message

Jesus said, "Let not your heart be troubled: you believe in God, believe also in me. In my Father's house are many mansions; if it were not so, I would have told you. I go to prepare a place for you. And if I go and prepare a place for you, I will come again, and receive you unto myself; that where I am, there you may be also."

JOHN 14:1-3

"Give me your hand and we'll take that journey you've been hearing about.

I'm so happy to finally hear from you. I was so concerned because I'd sent several messages to you by some of my trusted friends. I'd asked them to tell you how much I love you and how much my FATHER wants you to come back home...and now you're here. I am so pleased. Those messengers, who stopped by with the GOOD NEWS, are like I said, my dear friends. As friends, we spend a lot of time together. They listen to me, they learn from me. As a matter of fact, I taught them how to pray for you. It works!

Where are we going? , you ask. We're going to my Father's house. It is beyond anything you could ever imagine. In my Father's house are many mansions, and one of them is yours. When will we get there? Well, remember this is a journey that may take a little while but I promise we'll get there, soon.

Are you ready? Then give me your hand. Hold on tightly because the way is quite narrow. The road can get a little rocky sometimes, but don't worry because I'll never leave you nor forsake you. You must trust me always especially when it's very dark and you can't see, then you must let my eyes be your eyes. You'll go many places and do a lot of things. I have so many good things to teach you. You must refer to your guide Book all the time because it has vital instructions to keep you on track.

Sometimes I'll take you up to the mountain and you'll feel the soft wind and bright light of the SON on your face...you'll like that so much you'll want to stay. But we'll have to come down where we'll sometimes find ourselves in the valley and even in some dry and thirsty places. Along the way we'll find a quiet stream and rest and refresh ourselves with living water. This world can get so noisy and chaotic that you'll need a place where you can hide out. It's during those quiet times that we'll fill ourselves with the peace and the joy that only comes from our Father. That's a feeling you won't quite understand!

You'll have to make many stops on this journey. You see, now that you're my friend, you must tell your family, your friends and acquaintances about me. Why, you'll even tell people you don't know about me. Give them the same message that you heard. They may never hear unless you tell them. Don't worry about what to say, just tell them you have some good news they're *dying* to hear about. Remember I'll be with you to help you always.

A word of caution! Always look straight ahead at me. You may be distracted and get thrown off track. You'll be tempted to take a short cut or go the route you think is better than what your *map* says. You might even want to stop because of the bumps in the road. There is also someone on the road who hates the fact you're walking with me. He is evil and will use all kinds of tricks to make you think this journey is really not worth all the effort. He'll play with your mind and try to convince you that you can't make it. When those times come (and they will come), just remember to think like me, act like me, be like me. If you should get tired and sit down or even if you stumble and fall, quickly let the Father know and He'll pick you up.

Oh yes, you must have the right clothes for the journey. Your outfit is a special military uniform that I've already bought for you. Here, put it on and keep it on, **all the time**. Just in case you hadn't figured this out yet, the road we're on is like a battleground; it's war, but guess what? I won the war over 2,000 years ago and my victory is your victory. You just **stand** ready in position with your weapon aimed, and I'll do the fighting. Remember that!

So, are you ready?...then come and go with me to my Father's house."

About the Author

Renee Hill Carter is on staff at Nations Ford Community Church in Charlotte, NC, where she serves as Executive Coordinator to the Senior Pastor. An encourager, she is an Associate Minister involved in teaching and counseling.

A graduate of Hampton University, Hampton, Virginia, Mrs. Carter worked in Marketing for 17 years in the telecommunications industry before joining the staff of her church. She also has a Masters Degree in Christian Counseling from Queen City Bible College, Charlotte, NC.

A native of Beckley, West Virginia, she and her husband, Bill (William), reside in Charlotte, NC. They are the parents of three adult children; a son, William Jr. (Keith), two daughters, LaKeshia Landrum (husband Mitchell) and LaChanda; and at this writing, two amazing grandchildren, Mitchell, Jr. and Kamryn Landrum.

Ordering Information

If you were blessed and encouraged by these inspired writings, bless and encourage someone else.

"A Good Work Begun" is internationally distributed and can be purchased at Amazon.com and other worldwide outlets in print or e-book version.

The audio version of "A Good Work Begun" can be found at all digital sites (iTunes, Amazon.com, CDBaby.com, etc.) Listen to the words spoken by the author set to music designed to calm and soothe your soul.

Visit www.mulberryhousecreations.com. Both the print version and CD of "A Good Work Begun" are available.

Discover an array of other inspirational products at Mulberry House Creations that will enlighten, encourage and touch the very heart and soul.

Greeting Cards by A Write Touch™

Touch the heart of that special someone through beautifully designed cards for any occasion. Customize the thoughts you wish to convey through the stroke of a pen. Leaving a personally hand-written note is the thoughtful and considerate way to express how you truly feel.

P. O. Box 19673
Charlotte, NC 28219-9798
www.mulberryhousecreations.com
carterrh@aol.com

My Father In Heaven

My Father On Earth

By S Lynn G

Copyright © 2010 by S Lynn G

My Father In Heaven My Father On Earth
by S Lynn G

Printed in the United States of America

ISBN 9781604770377

All rights reserved solely by the author. The author guarantees all contents are original and do not infringe upon the legal rights of any other person or work. No part of this book may be reproduced in any form without the permission of the author. The views expressed in this book are not necessarily those of the publisher.

Unless otherwise indicated, Bible quotations are taken from The King James Version of the Bible. Copyright © 1990 by Thomas Nelson, Inc.

www.xulonpress.com